EACH OF US (OUR CHRONIC ALPHABETS)

Natasha Cuddington

EACH OF US (OUR CHRONIC ALPHABETS)

ARLEN
HOUSE

Each of us (our chronic alphabets)

is published in 2018 by
ARLEN HOUSE
42 Grange Abbey Road
Baldoyle, Dublin 13, Ireland
Phone: 353 86 8360236
arlenhouse@gmail.com
arlenhouse.blogspot.com

Distributed internationally by
SYRACUSE UNIVERSITY PRESS
621 Skytop Road, Suite 110
Syracuse, NY 13244–5290
Phone: 315–443–5534
Fax: 315–443–5545
supress@syr.edu
syracuseuniversitypress.syr.edu

ISBN 978–1–85132–203–9, paperback

Typesetting by Arlen House

Cover artwork: 1528 Parhelia over Innsbruck/Nebensonnen über Innsbruck *and* 1549 Parhelia and sword/Nebensonnen und Schwert, *The Book of Miracles/Das Wunderzeichenbuch,* c. 1545–1552, unattributed

LOTTERY FUNDED

CONTENTS

ACKNOWLEDGEMENTS

My thanks to the editors of journals and anthologies in which versions of these poems first appeared: *4x4, Washing Windows? Irish Women Write Poetry,* and to Eiléan Ní Chuilleanáin at *Cyphers.*

To Eilish Martin for her continued insight, and to Ruth Carr for her collaboration in all of its forms.

To Damian Smyth and the Arts Council of Northern Ireland for their support in the making of this work.

Thank you to Alan Hayes for his fealty to women's poetries on this island.

from

PARHELIA

In This   Disclosure of Reeds

Walk a field /

    Against its boundary

How it is Worried in-

to setts of Badger Steps of Moose Coyote Skeleton

line& it Has   Fingers

zenith a gloaming   it proceeds

In constituent

                                         where

Boys feed Hair

 w / Feathers

              Drawn Outside Our Reach

              Such a region of Trees /

If I were Deaf you Would Forgive me Blind&

Cannot See

Boy without His   cap

Barehead   Fortuitous

          In Coming Night /

Twilight That is Night Because of its Promises

Flare& éclat   In a wave of Mountain,

          Ours, though We Had

Not Imagined   it

And cast a Parenthetic Ark

Ten years on this road / to round Each Street

Gaze at Hills, yr. Black mountain:

Not What Mountain lookslike

Is not /

a robin.

We
       Have men,

Ambling a path of our streets

           Small Hours /

&Wish to Pass Nigh estranged

Acquaintances

      relief

We have Men.

Bereaved of Dawn's   equanimity

Day to mete out&

 And from it:

        We Notify /

   light:

        How it is come and Beats,

        Likely by Shadows&

        Plausible /

By Night

What you Fault /

Region of my grass& Dream

Way Sun reaches its   Plea

To

Tint a willing Mind

Same sea separates me

its Wrought edge

 Cannot make Shade from

        nadir,

Moment /

lift its Tonsure   Head to Speak

Never Has any Colour

Keener More Ardent

Together Withers   the arms

        Mingles with a

Fog& Verdigris /

Mounted against Civic Halls dimday Assembly

Stations,

Cyan Painted Plate

Tin Grate

Green What mars Green /

    recognition Meaning is Covered

    Past-Use

    Too late

EyeletEye

Sun gathers up the hook

Arc& carapace

      Trees Cut Out again

      House What /

      Home Built

Like Woman   in   Whose Past

Boy is Electrocuted Mislaid to a Creek Yes

Once the House Were White&

And from a Train

Another Kind of   mastery Just

Having Been There

Stones /

Same Sea /

 Bald Grace begot   Too a Breast / of Waves

Sons Their Blue Eyes,

When you Have Left

When   I

        When
at

    Seas / There May be Burials When Laws

        are flouted (when at seas

Eyes I Keep&

                           I am Penitent /

To Shorn her Hair

a Sheep in Spring

          Natural self

asunder

          Bald& Infectious Certain Straight sight

Houses' long abandon

Egg-shape   paint&

Wind / that Eats /

        This Blessed   burning,

Not Fallow Fire Fire Antipodal

        dogged Jump that licks

and Eats

Rain,

Though Hill gestures   Mountain

Wan   And Every Corner Tour Guides Sing

  Audible & not Heard

                              refract backlight
a scattering

                                        parhelion

prairie   Itself Prime /

from

GRACE

torn from its Circle

Where we abduct our sons.

Slaughter   a latched gates&

Lay Place This Lightsome /

           Ring of   Morning

AFTER the glister

of cumulus& Smell like wheat /

Raven at lowtide His single rock or

legendary Soul disgracious Impudent

Enough to

Shoulder This   His   monument

thee

Who Need not be motif

Mine   Mean

                                         to   Flight

NIGHTENGALE a pigeon

Who

Can not fly

Who is Not Flying /

Hastens its step

Mine Own awkward glide

all us our trespasses

                allayed by a

tide /

          When Thieves arrive Take their Bounty &

Break Us in the windless

        Caul

NOWDAYS kids don't Touch

Pay their filial bond&

Play

Their fervent ardours /

By Way of jewel or Sequined

　　Headphones.

we know

    the sour That   happens /

  (& as   Handkerchiefs /
   let fly

  Unnerved, recalcitrant

  To the Flame.

CONJOINED in glittering

Contract&

Waves that share

Their /

 Pulse against in bodies'

        chime)

we know

empathy&

the formation of a Closed   unit,

its capacity Struck.

IS pigeons /

Lost their perches

Sea and crag they Once graced&

Populate   the transom Windows of Europe,

Safety

                WE

Make   Wild

                            of

understand it Eyes we know   His

Own /

For Whom corsairs&   barbarypirates Could not

Wait Birthed at sea to Hoy Him Seed

Across

EYES

that / Sightless blinds

To Input "Lambeth slaves" posits Ariel Castro   phantasm

"not

  monster,"

  Screenburn phosphorus &

glitzy

    Flocked by its ghost /

Gracegraced with a flexed Blaze of

destiny, its pillars and Forewarnings   its

ardent

Namesake

FESTOONED& demurred

Like Injury / to the skull Acts of suicide

Auto-erotics Otherwise

Thee Hung aubadeastride the   Family

Shrine

grace

      coupled   to the Balk /

    Your Father's face yr. First shape-

shifting&

  dissent,

        follicles Whitescalp to   Constellate

    the grisly Jettisoned   Heart

BECAUSE it takes a body

to regret /

Such violent Slights&

Machines to revive Any

Connectivity When the Flash news story /

Brings you to your Knees Beats raw

Infamy

fact&   the Faceted /

Heart Bovine canticles /

White quartz on the Hill,

                              Its   Own chanted

vitriol:

DAWN'S bulletin: Three /

Caged / Women

Neighbours who we also know

                                                            to
Believe

        Luck Monsters fly-by-night passerines /

VirginsSaints

Who came by coracle Quit by cabbage Leaf

her /

Father's Daughter's

Face

WE also know Boy Himself

Becomes coupled /

            Place its patrimonies And That boys

Themselves Can be fused Together,

  sylph-like /

            Between Incident&

care

white kerchiefs

cavort   an rince mór /

Burren illumined by the

        shirts of

                Men

HIS spit facsimile

Daughter In Whose image /

Daughter Whose   daughter

Soaked&Plangent on grandmother's arm,

four knife cuts to Her neck

        And

 Out into the

                Street

stripped of their Blankets

White-tailed&

fallow /

Deer

MOTHER slaked&

Muddy /

Her wounded wrist& necks

a   very Knife the

Clotted filigree

 His Beatings /

mothers' delicately distended noses,
shoulders' fracturefractured filaments,

and cannonball, What Slit /

ground Beneath her feet,

Yet did not Make Her

fall.

ARIEL'S   terminal

    Facebook   entry "Miracles

do

Happen, God is good"   One day   before Other

Birth-days /

    With Whom he sat Eating ribs /

    At the Neighbourhood

barbeque,

sleight& facility Net a shroud

Any /

            slab at the Chancel Garlanded by arrows /

But Swine fodder

     Grace

WE know joints recover,

Fractures cleave& make Haste

But a coupled Admixture,

Leaves its

Composite

Trace /

harry by Three Arrows&

galley men now   Horseback   Birds

Her Stag / Fallen   off

a Flat World

ONE beseeched by puppies

What prevents Another from speedily Turning

 Away /

Her brown Eyes&

fused pubescence

Because /

There are snares a morass

For Which We are lured

how it fell for the Murder Holes&

licked mounting Waves

like shine / Grace her best galley affixed to the bed

by glinting Hole   a

Citadel

WHITEROCK

Wan& milk   the torque-edge bent of

roof

metal,

 not verdigris but Shine /

A Backlit cloud, or Course

of gulls

Who Hold trajectory in Common

light&

capability   That

            dialect   of light /

        First And the fist of   first

        Breaking /

        Through

WHAT makes an autonomy,

 Saint-like /

Has She   acted a Monster

Upon circumstance

                Care is taken   from us

 First,

        Beyond repair,

a Hastening /

a   Doubt.

desire exultantdesire

GIRLS torn together

Hot flush of Man's sex / Superlative need

Having Presented itself in idiom

argot   of Capture&   fettering
At puberty   Given Such

        a plastic Heart /

Translucent   glittering Worn cri de Coeur Like its

        subject a replica

times I am the moment

its raft of crucibles /

                                                            Talk-
Shows&

Telepathic Misfits Who recuperate the Dead

                                                            girls /

Vanquished under Water Omphalos

                                                            grace

ONE gave birth in plastic /

Pool so as that Chaos of blood

were easily clean&

dungeon /

Where Humans wring of you its citizen

Water was There

a

Colour of Eyes&

finialgap a foramen I cast   doubt /

A Sea between fact& dignity.

                              Years /

One floats & Is   doubt.

Is No sense of Adventure,

          Failure to do   Otherwise.

AND Cold of the Basement

were punishment

                              Heat /

of the loft castigation&

Now the   seasons

Grieve

those   who

have known Desire&

Act

    judiciously   Upon
    it

WHEN Woman mislaid Beauty

Shorn   Her Hair&

Radius of her Cheek-

bone

shattered into   an archipelago

We are Human Animal /

What

antecedents

children

 We fling Will Across

Our

         Unanswered Fury With

         wings /

WE KNOW we have Man

Departed

days / after His obligatory tins&

Left untaken from the Porch His

Monstrous Indignities pissed at dawn on

Cider,

Igniting

our jetsam
for Warmth

a Fatal& auspicious /

semaphore

AND THOUGH

we are aghast& filled w / avarice

His Monster will not Longer Walk

Beside Us This

Streets

whose ambitions Make amusement-

  parks High Speed rides& rollercoaster trains

So Boys can ride&

      And be Pulled (back) to Us,

         a thousand selfsame sentence of

Their life /

                plus   its grief

CORNER or perpendicularity

Look don't

Look /

as the Crowd   gathers&

Barefisted fighters Stage Their   theatre at the street

Where peopled, vacant cars

Where Plumb batons&

aplomb   bars

mountains hatched Then Hacked against veils of

walls of

Blue grief

SON LOOK at us Not One

To peer through /

The shattered Window Not

Even This

  Shock of   Morning /

Flourish Gulls or sun Makes

  Us   Anything Other

Than what We

                are

blest like carrion

      Transmutes itself /

Of Danger   Flees its Own White Tail&

That Dark

        hour's

lament (at) dawn

WHEN Deer /

Shot by   po-lice

 It will not Be Tranquilized

Ruts his gridiron   Slumps

(to) Defter pogroms,

Gulls locked in equipoise /

polyesternylon mist-

        nets&

animals' endangered /

grace

animal Grace dead deer arrayed at the

Wings /

of brigand piracy

WHERE lights Amber

Encumber   the amble

of /

  Old Tides,

        Ravens gather

To speak to us of Night Heron&

 Us that we are not

Wolves

PRINT

at the dawn of the moon of paper

a tip-edge of fascicle,

I pitch the handroller on its axis / Await

That euphony of ink on plate,

sand on seed on seed of Sand

Alchemy of matter

What Whispers at Birds&

tree

Make themselves

legible

unlike this poem, For Which there is beginning&

no end,

fact of the artifact is not re-

                            capitulated.

Print is proofed And

set again, quoins tightened loosed w / their key

But Once pigment, its soiled finger   kiss

 that page

          into the Hereafter,

beginning at the chambered cases,

Wonder at sons' unwieldy will:

will too, they dip to frisk Each socket /

's estranged type

sepulchral and confetti   in the inverse cupola

Of a small hand&

streaked with a precept of ink upon ink

And   cyan

disquiet detonates to

 Will.

Fridays their purpose,

          to edge across impasto cotton&   conceive /

again what doesn't Matter: Indian or Somerset

Each / a hand's pace / beat of   sense What Says:

Ease is what's made.

this mark cannot be Changed

You squander and slight Skill. That mollifies will. That is

assuaged.

you Begin /

to   Know what work is.

And this Ordering of paper, tally of the run,

is a sequestering&

Capacity   made out of range,

sometimes to birdsong,

                    Never a melancholy

Wind: That lifts the

                    Print to dash upon itself,

And you (to) lunge at this strange music,

(a   Measure from its wing.

and Battered cotton of a thousandsleepssheets /

preserved in stack-forms

to ripshred& douse

with Spirits.

On print day,

When Boys are to school&

Men work, I come to Labour Mine / That is not   Theirs,

glad-rags exchanged for utility, Tied with cord.

go bare-eyed to the composing stick:

Nearsight is best. Worry numbedthumbs to nimble

form.

not Tea or / tincture, the stainless rule&

Thumbscrew Catch graphemes

to site And&

Though I plot& Measure Lay the wooden Furniture

Said   Eye

rend quoins strip the screw

a Pressure of / constraint /

       Each dam of space   form&

       forme shored w / card,

          Let the set line Scatter

         arc of craft it builds in Air

Mind's fingers (cascading leadfounttype abandon keys

And begin Again.

though a Print

           finds itself& the Poem its end

           said printing

Is not Done. For

 Image /

increases itself in the World, Motif sharpens (to) the

Mind's maladroit

                Finger.

we Harken More intricate filigree.

Whence the critical Eye

descends /

Notices all undone&

Posterity

Held / in the shape of shape of a

Hand.

the mislaid   letter, the lost

      Case

the gentle interstice   loosed from Itself /

through an open window

skimmed or overprinted over.

          Unless torn or

Dynamite,

remains.

  Unlike, surely / by dint of white

        Weather, endangered&

    Sun-bright on the backs of Mislaid gulls /

this leafless   arc of lucent trees

render of our humanhomes

at the cold bone of January

&
 knowing now the Hold a gauge pin

          Can have on   range /

Paper the way its frame holds view /

And Through   (said) window,

Compose year's bleak   Oblivion.

often you wish the walls to break

the way They did for youth /

      Where possibility

Was all and a location.

Other times / Wonder if to content one-

self the knowing limbs of Children One Bound

 delimited space,

                      Grace Within

that simple

          Happiness.

in the bone of winter,

 Robin roosts at my newel

          post /

As I   rise / stairs to work We both Know what day

                              it will be,

      Hour(s) the white-breath

Earth Lays Dense its   rememory

              across
              view

let your birds back

into their hiding Homes /

   flight, their clustering

   Curiosities,

Await That place of wood& paper cotton

     Nature

is trying to Make Itself voluble&

glowing withinwithout your   Open room

world where sons have no byname /

for that   face of Letter,

On Which Public Marks are / made& Whom

this missive's for.

Worry its largesse:

prize of foldedarrow sign and facets dispatch place&

Hand /

Having been there.

with plaintive bonefolder, feel the Mind's curve

     contriving /

 Page   to page

      s

 arch of cow-leg to Hand. What

 Divides thought(s) from Thought

plane from plane ruffled deckle-edge from   crease,

fence from cut from rule from End.

rather than, a solution of parts) sand as seed or seed

of grain Alphabet   as matrix for granule   phonemes /

  The scrawled Shape as object

  Not locomotive expression,

        Self.

              yourself you must enact Everything,

skins of ink / on plate letters

that lace a page (that Lace of page /

      Thought's face(s)

      facing page.

and when the world forgets you

I will swell in infinite gesture /

Seed at the seat of your   Hand

The sorrow of your   record,

Zephyr   Eye

vowel of water apologue what fashions itself

towardsinward

Aa / ox in which Beloved landscape lies

and when if sorrow

falls on tinkered keys   Case

will lead the upper chamber /

          Where mice are   Heard,

domestic shades& small machines   succumb

tree in weed-wind

  Marks Intricacy your delicate constituencies all

before there was pause /

Aristophanes of Byzantium

fugitive& Overcome in the gush of Text

His Votive Points hew verse   breath

                              Periodos
   komma

kolon

            Before there was typography /

            To Carve the shape of sound   obscenity

candour) the curvilinear)   Oo
line cast back on Itself / made apparition,

   Apparent and explosive thing.

in the shade of Black Mountain

lastgasp winter's plastic flags spurn gulls& bees

      Luminary   Winter

     barren gorse or thatch of tree /

        Make a white flag of paper, abandoned thing

        an exegesis /

Hood of tree Mark its measures   capacity   Talk

Tree of / itself Seeds' indelible frangible creed.

excepting ink's patina /

On the body   of type

What bears marks) becomes a peril to practice,

Form.

Table galley roller mallet

Rasp& shine / Make like you Have never been,

dark Blot obliged to apparatus a   machine.

now with the   imaged,

Horse's bit /

      a spoke both green and broken

Unlock the bridledmechanism to place,

 furlough where you Carry from

        And hold to Breath   in That litter of phonemes /

 World slows to a drawl

&

moment drives its emboss, patterning in.

if you could turn back

from Wind / If paper could Know /

      despite any   dispensation

      Best-suited to the systems of a Printer's bench,

There is   domestic Habit What throws   type Its feet&

Handle obstructed its lack of   fluency /

      the gulp above the air it seems to Swallow,

shining back   of morning.

                And just like that   is truant,

Type to   case / Unpicked at speed Need

 or need to intone& trill

            By sleet / That washes snow, Day intrudes

Know That you will not find

   Concealment necessary to

Begin Again.

in the winter / never bothers
with the supposition of End,

       Trees glance&

break / Branches point a structure of veins / Of   ink-
blown breath across a page,

       Also entanglements of feeling

Each time you work. Hold /

             the rule conversance can steady,

Hands   Becoming Themselves.

as Tt marks a spot / rock

Wall (on which you began (to

Make the   Tree of your Hand.

white dog&   all   space,

tryst w / sun or winter's white Mothering,

all blanket silence Consistencies.

Winds That crawl   at the ear taw tau te / mark turned End

phonogram pictogram a memory skewed by   usage

it is all over sister you never had Promise of a winter's end.

      Almost on purpose Sun beats its pledge /

      at birds and Their   wings,

  the explicit face of type,

  occluded   Mountain   view

  Through trees

Which just now air their butchered limbs

to Begin.

over, the directionless fret&

directed   wonder

          Tympan's depth / bite of face

steep deboss cutting push from platen.

What is legible, not / strict blade

          A Printmaker associates this rule,

steadies page against   its Metal:

  Tear but Never   cut,
  Give paper its deckle Remind back the   Mould.

with a sick child Awaits& you /

On the end of a tethering

Who would rather   sit with the tympan,

its gauge   Between us (align a run in orderly queue

If Litany   wind turbine rollers over ink

Draws to an edge is paper story Without declension,

if spring bird is arrival& escape Then Wonder

was never Enough

through walls that is not walls

Trick of nascent hills

cloud or breath caught in the eye

you know things Finer /

That mouldmade affects its Handmade by machine.

But the hand Holds fibre & fount Meet They etch together

foolishly   Cast themselves back at meaning.

the way line   began

matchless horizon Hours before grass   wheat
  Rise to challenge consequence,

     Where boundary intuits freely in a bluff of trees /

     Now Cities' fracture /

These

     Suit   a poem fine the frame   8 x 5
altogether (limitless   range Such Happinesses even

          freedom

rain   of blackthorn, whose

      Paper I bring in   confetti

to stud table and surface all /
like whits of   birch Collected& abandoned to this

House / you will   print

      this

      Bark, where fugitives lie its upper reaches&

      superstition animal   Tradition

Remains.

little bird(s) of fretful energy,

      wasps that climb / a leaf   Heap

      as soon as you are still.

In the blind   deboss of   Mood,

 Light fills a space with ambition

you will return the stairs as this new season

winter returns to rattle its corner

Who   Heard of snow

so close in spring now

inflorescence makes its Own / Snow&

it is not virtual, it is real

This planet's

Hatred of us all that is new tenderling

there is still, print of bird

on a roof / visible   from this window,

      Murdered from its tree.

Like   Tree (in once it   perched

How pruned Within& fossil-

like felicitously contorted / pictogram to alphabet Before
our

      looking   Eyes.

we want it to communicate something.

if technique distorts Sun   blanches too long to the past,

There is one tailfeather&

traces of a   symmetry /

Neat part loosed but clinging

Visage   coheres / a body its feet Ours

wormwind Takes (it arches its wings

if you wait long enough

they alight& quote their code /

        If print day is   Missed,

      balance the cusp of light And season

      Hour(s) moving forward, like the Hand

  detecting   its youth.

Not quite you are weight of tadpole dormant bulb

      Wading in.

at precipice of blossom

lay of the case / also considered,

       Upper& Lower   devised in our   minds

       by that tendency of capital letter to sit High in   its

            chamber /

            Like cherries' first blossoms /

Whose proximity to high air And Sun declares Their

                         Imperious

symbol in space   to Everyone.

winter makes its last dash against (the   hope of trees

Whose blossom is marker but also Heel.

we make   fleet sparks to the world /

Be   Slow

on the Cases burn small these bright fires Type you pick&

Return.

you forget how coloured eggs are

broken from their   tree

       Wind or (magpie) birds whose Black and white

           dangles   across /

  Page /

             Whose Paper we have struck Beat

from Trees   to pulp and bleed our scriptura continua,

mercifully interpointed / speckled joints   a style

on the day the fox arrives

spring has laid   its furniture

        trees fuss branches' impetus with buds' insistent

form.

  Fox Who has come (from Hills that are   not mountains,

  By river / to slake a thirst Things easy& Human,

        Minds you to move in space /

move   and move on.

when fox has called the door

is not longer motif its progeny   skitter

the days that fall   between

      Houses /

           And Print themselves

genderless& agrestal on this

           field (built by   Hands,

size will bend the story,

Wonder genus or species   to a burning

Overprint this small yard / on a park on Black Mountain

a concealed river& wildness that has brought

Fox   to you /

And you   to Here.

and you could carve the fox

the way you carved the bird

       You could   tape the rails /

to glance that block's hard wood   discern

earthly currencies day wellspent,

      a speckled egg Their speech all proem& preamble

        Older Than   (ours

in the garden fox is animal

you know   from the window / of a small room

  Like the press its feat is usage Until Grace

                                        occludes it

                          When you print in rhythm&

          Time   Marks trees' scoured   surface

letter Ff voiceless fricative at the lip And Teeth /

fox Sounds mud with Hooks or

clubs   of legs

window you are not to reveal

that they put in / what is set   to bring

  Light

  in which, is tended   park& margin a violence

Held by the witness of Mountain,

trees' fire-ash Wish   that bodies were smoke& air

anywhere   Other than freedom

the blossom is dead and keening

itself / not kanji or poundstore   serene.

             Cannot be Attached   to us,

But Feint /

  Interiority fulmination from Marrow

                to mordant Flesh litters the blackish gutters

overfull (overflows   the street

its flushed sheets not   material

gatefold, bevel or wove /

to billet petty metaphor Insolences   our grief

Limbs pinpoint Wake greylight

vocables at a mass frontier   communications

Where Hands tear gilt-edge,

flatter humanity.

when imprint of fox that fox

has made

dies from cache&

spring's other insurgencies /

polis, conurbations (civility Haggard

Shock of (being)   Other&

stained the wove of solitude

if you could open   the door

any sentient thing /

          issue orison Befall the jointed palm of leaf

Now Seething from a want of   sun /

bequest of a reminder

          That Mouth moves to touch

                              pariah And the lecherous,

text is this currency

through the ink slab

patina or shadow What Hands   scavenge

      from calibration&
tensity

        yes letters are pictures /

Kk an outstretched hand Air of lung& diaphragm

things their voiceless   phonations   bone-carved glyph

 bleeding

               charge

like iris strayed from the eye of Oo

The hieroglyph for   Hand /

       set to Kk's value   by a word in a language

(merged with its sound,

           So Alphabets /

    Steal their ways to dominance,

      efficacy poised at the open-hand   of logogram

like worn mallet or round bodkin

serif flaunts the resolution of   stroke

    Symbols Fitted to an evangelical zeal

    for origin its   ornament /

  Flare& light   of Hand,

daubed then carved to neaten End Where letter   began

its numberless projections

what I have known to be gilt-edge(d)

increased   in pace its marquetry,

dwam of systems / Stain across the case

Newly muscled arm   Which knows

How letters use their words /

are set against themselves or left   blunt&

attenuated, Hare sighted   Hawk from above

and drawn   their thread from form

way the dead bird   leaves its print

on the Mood of my sons /

Whose letters   are paws&

Ink   of blackfeather (manus folded / into a fluttering

overhead   the complect branching of wings.

what they know about weather

pressed   to the field of a Hand.

          Cheated & flexed to a symmetry /

Each   of us (our chronic alphabets,

      Waking Night &

              gesture
 at
Trees (give their shapes to the window (without cover

PARHELIA

Wonted to prairie winter, parhelia manifest as near spheres that flank the sun. Their pomp is mirage made by light refracted in hexagons of ice that decorate the aerosphere. As the vernacular *sundog* suggests, parhelia withdraw from their greatest lambency at the horizon as the sun ducks an exigent angle. They dog the setting sun to night.

At Scandza, parhelia were limned as *solhund* dog and *solvarg* wolf. They tracked sun as tails of cirrus or cirrostratus swathed dawn or dusk. In what is now Saskatchewan, sundogs are descried by Plains Cree as a sign of cold, and *ka nemiskotawehtet pîsim* the sun walks bearing its own campfires. Chapters of the *Jinshu* cite 'Ten Haloes' on which *jih-shu* might superimpose themselves as sign apropos to an emperor-sun. Greeks viewed the *parēlion* as a boding of storms and listed visitations in poems like Hesiod's *Works and Days* and the prose of Eudoxus in *Mirror* and *Phainómena*, and Aristotle's *Meterologica*. Versified by Aratus, *Phainómena* forewarns us to mark '[880]Marks as the Sun is rising or setting, whether the clouds, called parhelia, blush (on South or North or both), nor make the observation in careless mood.' Across medieval Europe, parhelia were figured in art as omen of the edict of Christian God. Whatever lexicon, they colour beholders with a surety that changing conditions are due.

That they should arrive in pairs is salient to long poem. As the mind bends experience, approaches metaphor, there is no simple geometry. There is the wanton replica. In a vastness or plains, a compositional expanse, there is the *klōn* or twig of subject in a holt of possibility. There is a shape of thought that tracks itself to vanish at its most bright. If we are honest to the pulse of impulse, we say it is protean and recurs as conditions are right in the air. Meaning is not sculpted but gathers with fidelity.

There is also image which is never only itself but also its refractions through the crystal of memory. A mountain is never only a mountain. A bird is a bird but shows to us its many pairs of wings.

GRACE

Against what P.J. Joyce called 'the violent savage vandalism' of the Tudor colonial project, Gráinne Ní Mháille [1530–1603] trapped herself at the vanguard of insurgency. Ó Máille legatee and conspicuous sea-captain, she was traced for English state papers but lost to *Annála na gCeithre Máistrí*.

Like any confection, she appears as afterthought or tart mnemonic in a discourse of Irish revolutionary. She is James Joyce's 'prankquean' 'her grace o'malice' and 'wild old grannewwail' – and trine of contrived femininity. She is available to us in any extant bodice-ripper or dance drama, street ballad or fantasy park.

Her manoeuvres include the close-cropping of hair and a period of cross-dress in youth. She invoked Brehon law to 'dismiss' her second husband and abducted a child of the Anglo-Norman peerage whom she ransomed for a bond of hospitality. She petitioned on behalf of her male sons at the court of Queen Elizabeth I in conjoint Latin fluency. She disposed of a handkerchief to a fire as was her custom at the twilight of its possibility. She was igneous and conflagrant to the narrative of savage and civility.

Ariel Castro [1960–2013] was a bus driver for the Cleveland Metropolitan School District in Ohio. He was also a musician who 'played and owned many musical instruments including various types of guitars.' After a patterned violence against his common-law wife and the habitual kidnap of her daughters, he began abducting young women and incarcerating them at his home on 2207 Seymour Avenue.

On 6 May 2013 Amanda Berry fled with her daughter after a decade of starvation, sexual assault and mutual restraint. Gina DeJesus and Michelle Knight gained liberty in a rescue by police. Michelle Knight had been effaced from the National Crime Databank fifteen months after vanishing. Amanda Berry and Gina DeJesus had materialized on *Oprah*

Winfrey and *Montel Williams* where a psychic alerted that Berry was exanimate and 'in water'.

Ariel Castro was found hung by bedclothes one month after being sentenced to life imprisonment without parole plus 1,000 years. Hypotheses evince accidental death by auto-erotic asphyxiation or suicide. In rangy testimony, Castro stated that 'To be a musician and to be a monster I don't think I can handle it … Like I said, I drove a school bus, I'm a musician, I had a family.' The FBI describes a handwritten letter in which Castro states that he was sexually abused as a child. His home was unbuilt in 2013.

PRINT

The poem was typeset by hand in Centaur and letterpressed in an edition of 16. Foundry Centaur was crafted letter by each letter. Its serif and modulation belong to each glyph. As per Robin Bringhurst in *The Elements of Typographic Style,* 'Cutting letters by hand – like writing them by hand – makes repetition all but impossible.' However diminutive, Bringhurst tenders that we detect such rhythms visually. They mark us with the intuition that endeavour is conspicuous.

Devised as titling capitals for the Metropolitan Museum of Art, Centaur was expanded by Bruce Rogers for the George B. Ives translation of Georges-Maurice de Guérin's *Le Centaure*. It takes its humanism from a Eusebius fount 'cut at Venice' by French typographer Nicolas Jenson in 1470. Centaur's purchase was proposed to me by Roy Caslon. He knew, like Bringhurst and Rogers, that Centaur's grace had thew to petition the hand.

Eric Gill vexes the poem. His controversy shined on radio and *Ariel between Wisdom and Gaiety* proliferated. This inevitable passage from *Autobiography*:

> The shapes of letters do not derive their beauty from any sensual or sentimental reminiscence. No one can say that the o's roundness appeals to us only because it is like that of an

apple or of a girl's breast or of the full moon … Letters are things, not pictures of things.

Gill is conjured in Black Dog's *Alphabets, A Miscellany of Letters*. Doubting Gill's dictum, David Sacks says: 'letters, in their Bronze Age origins, *used to be* pictures. Our capital letter shapes – most of them – began as pictures. Their shapes exist today as remembrances of pictures.' This essay's text is interposed with plates. Among them, an image of the 'eye' hieroglyph from which O takes its iris, A inverted as ox's head, figures of the sleight of K from a hieroglyph for hand. A debt also to a 1958 edition of *Printing Made Easy: A Comprehensive Instruction Manual; Arrestingly Written in Non-Technical Style for Users of ADANA Printing Machines.*

The poem is, for the most part, at its first gesture. It is piebald kits in the garden. It rehearses when, as per Georges-Maurice de Guérin – here as translated by T. S. Moore – 'In those days, too, I have cut branches in the forest, that, while running, I held above my head.'

Natasha Cuddington was born in Saskatchewan, Canada, and lives in Belfast. She has taken degrees in Creative Writing from Concordia University, Montreal (BA) and Irish Studies at Queen's University, Belfast (MA). Her translations, reviews and poems have appeared variously in journals and magazines. She has received grant awards from the Arts Council of Northern Ireland, including an ACES Award in 2011. In 2017 she was announced as recipient of the Ireland Chair of Poetry Bursary.

For ten years, she was a member of Word of Mouth Poetry Collective. With Gráinne Tobin she compiled the Collective's archive and deposited it at Belfast's Linen Hall Library. With Ruth Carr she curates the literary reading series *Of Mouth*, which published a posthumous collection of poetry by Ann Zell in 2016.